W9-DDJ-268

Leanne Grechulk

iUniverse, Inc.
New York Bloomington

30 Days to Wealth



The information, ideas, and suggestions in this book are not intended to render professional advice. Before following any suggestions contained in this book, you should consult your personal accountant or other financial advisor. Neither the author nor the publisher shall be liable or responsible for any loss or damage allegedly arising as a consequence of your use or application of any information or suggestions in this book.

iUniverse books may be ordered through booksellers or by contacting:

iUniverse
1663 Liberty Drive
Bloomington, IN 47403
www.iuniverse.com
1-800-Authors (1-800-288-4677)

Because of the dynamic nature of the Internet, any Web addresses or links contained in this book may have changed since publication and may no longer be valid. The views expressed in this work are solely those of the author and do not necessarily reflect the views of the publisher, and the publisher hereby disclaims any responsibility for them.

ISBN: 978-1-4502-5400-7 (pbk)
ISBN: 978-1-4502-5401-4 (cloth)
ISBN: 978-1-4502-5402-1 (ebk)

Printed in the United States of America

iUniverse rev. date: 9/29/2010

**LEGAL NOTICES:**



ISBN: 0-9866203-0-0

First Edition.

www.healthygirl.net

## HealthyGirl's 30-Day Wealth Transformation

**This book is published for the thousands of entrepreneurs-female, aspiring or otherwise-who seek a fuller, wealthier, and more energetic life. I have experienced firsthand the direct relationship between self-esteem and money and it is my hope that my 30-day program will inspire and remind you to unleash your creativity and expand your visionary process.**

**My program is proven to accelerate business success, personal excellence and wealth building. As you follow your 30-day program, remember to take good notes! This program is about expanding your personal awareness, to remind you that with all success comes failure. Don't get discouraged if you temporarily get off track. This program gives you permission to start fresh, to detach from old spending habits, and historical patterns.**

**Remember, money is a form of energy and as your wealth grows, your energy will too! As you learn and practice my strategies to building wealth, you will feel a sense of beautiful posture, self-confidence and personal power. Financial Freedom gives you multiple doorways to further tap into intuition, creativity, and contribution.**

A Few Things Before We Get Started:

1. To get the most out of this program, you will need to block some time out of your day; either in the morning or on your lunch hour over the next 30 days. Blocking 30-60 additional minutes before bed will also be required to succeed.

2. Purchase a copy of **Think and Grow Rich** by Napoleon Hill before starting the program.

3. Get your body ready for this program. Throughout the program, you will want to increase your water intake, take a

great multivitamin, exercise 4-5 times per week and take some time just for you each day. If you are seeking some advice or tips to keep your energy high and your health in check, a great article for you to read is **101 Ways To Have All The Energy You Want** by Jena la Flamme.

4. For each day during the program, read the 'section of the day' when you wake up in the morning, so that you know what your focus is for the day, and what activities you will need to complete before you go to bed.

5. You will clarify the following during your 30 day program:

    - Your vision

    - Your 30-day goal

    - Your financial freedom date (and how much per month that means for you)

6. And finally, please try to only read the section for the day you are on!

Let's Get Started!

Feeling Stuck?

I do not have an unfortunate set of circumstances that occurred where I was broke or homeless. I do not have anything dramatic to tell you. I was a great student; I came from a great family and had wonderful stability and security growing up. As I studied day after day through French elementary school, high school, and then university, I continued to feel emptiness in my life. Even at a young age, I could not figure out why anyone would want to spend an entire life studying, working, and retiring. It seemed sort of pointless to me. Like so many, I continued on my 'predestined' path, aimlessly and hopelessly going with the flow. I graduated from University with a B.Sc. in Biomedical Toxicology and then jumped right into the work force. I felt horrible each Sunday night getting ready for work, as I knew my life was lacking excitement and joy, and because I was not living my life's purpose. I continued on 'the path' by enrolling to do my MBA. At the time, I was working for a major pharmaceutical company and was also recently married. All was looking 'perfect' from the outside. People saw me as having a great job, a great house, great degrees and a great marriage. In the eyes of those around me, I was a great success. Sound familiar? The only problem was that I was unhappy and I spent many nights feeling as though I was living on autopilot. I simply was no longer satisfied with the depleting predictability of my day-to-day life. I knew the next step was having a family but I just felt like there was unfinished business for me to do. Nevertheless, I continued swimming upstream.

I cannot tell you what gave me the courage to wake up from autopilot mode. I simply had an emptiness inside that could no longer be pushed deeper. One day, I just decided to stop letting my life happen and start creating the life that I knew was waiting for me. The timing was right and I jumped in full force.

Four years later, I made a commitment and promise to myself that I would live each day with passion and purpose, because it was the only way I could live if I wanted to feel creative and fulfilled. Whatever challenges come my way; I would rather face them and enjoy the ride instead of living a life of quiet desperation. I did not want to settle!

This book is a 30-day system that brings together ten years of research, life experience, readings and strategies. I have interviewed several of today's top experts and authors including Olympic Gold Medalists, wealth experts, nutritionists, therapists, coaches, millionaires, authors and top entrepreneurs in order to compile the top 30 strategies for entrepreneurs who are seeking wealth and optimal health.

# Day 1 - Detox Your Life

Before you begin to create new things in your life, you must eliminate habits and mental clutter that keep you where you are today. To begin your 30-Day Wealth Program, it's time for a major declutter. A cluttered car, house, kitchen, and office equates to a seriously disorganized and cluttered mind. Without order, the mind cannot perform at its best and cannot create incredible success. In other words, to create a wonderful piece of art, you will need a blank canvas. Here's your homework for getting your life and mind in order: Clear out the mess!

- Kitchen Cupboard: Get rid of refined sugars, white flour, processed foods - all junk!

- Your Closet: Grab a garbage bag and fill it up with clothes, coats and shoes that do not fit or you have not worn in 12 months.

- Get rid of junk and knick-knacks around your home that create clutter.

- Write down all the activities, events, groups, and committees that you are on that are not aligned with your 2-3 year vision (we'll discuss on Day 2) or you do not feel empowered and excited to be a part of. Over the next two days, I challenge you to commit to taking these off your plate.

- Declutter and clean your office. Note: your desk should be clean and tidy!!! Get rid of papers, reminders, sticky notes and other junk messing up your desk and your mind.

- Declutter and clean your car (weekly!). Get it detailed! Get your car sparkling clean on a weekly basis.

Have you ever noticed that when you hop in the car of a successful person, their car is always clean and tidy? This is not a coincidence. A clean car reflects a clean and orderly mind. This is just one habit of a wealthy and successful entrepreneur!

I devote two hours every Friday afternoon to decluttering! I declutter my office, my car and any other area of my life that is chaotic or disorderly. Book two hours of declutter time each week into your calendar and watch what happens after a month of keeping these 'declutter' appointments. If your environment is a mess, your mind is a mess.

*My Life- Decluttered*

As I mentioned earlier, four years ago, I found myself completely starting over. New city, new job, new home, new life! I knew the way I operated in the past was no longer an option. My mind was in complete chaos with no focus and no clear vision. I was working all day, doing my MBA courses at night, and often after that, I would be working on my course assignments for the next day. That was all in addition to the emotional impact of going through a difficult time in my relationship. My mind and my life was a mess. I think at one point I had 6 empty bottles of diet coke (a bad habit I had for a very long time!), 3 pairs of shoes, my gym clothes, my yoga mat, 3 binders, 10 files, my MBA gear, my marketing plans, water bottles and much, much more in my car! It was honestly like a small country had taken up residence in my car. To make matters worse, I was a shopaholic and would frequently drop $1000 in an hour at a few of my favorite boutiques. My closet was so full that I forgot I even owned many of my brand new, never worn outfits. Needless to say, in this new chapter of my life, I was burnt out emotionally and physically and again, had no concrete or defined long-term vision.
Moving forward in this new chapter in my life, I was committed

to creating more inner and outer peace. I wasn't able to kick my diet coke habit easily (one of the toughest addictions to break might I add), but I did purge my life in major ways. I donated 12 bags of clothes and shoes to the Canadian Diabetes Association, kicked my perfectionist ways, gave closure to relationships that were no longer serving me and gave away or sold most of what I owned; so much so that a neighbour wondered if I was going through some type of early adulthood crisis. The interesting thing was that I had never felt so free and happy in my entire life. I was letting go of everything in my life that was 'good' so I could make room for the greatness that was to come. Month after month, I just kept removing and decluttering. Granted, I was single and had no children, so it was easy to live the life of a gypsy, and I have seen so many other women experience tremendous things after creating order in their lives.

Just the other day, the incredible woman who helps me with my housecleaning asked me how one person could have so little laundry each week. She compared my washing load with my boyfriend's washing load and we laughed over the difference. His 25 t-shirts per week compared to my four. I got so 'lean' in my clothing inventory that I did not even own a decent pair of winter shoes or boots. I may have taken my off-loading a little too far but it does feel great to be a minimalist…even for a week!

A lovely book that shares the value and steps to creating anything you want by decluttering your life is **Professional Dreamer** by Ghalil. A beautiful read!

There are also some great articles on HealthyGirl's website including **'Detox Your Life'** that you might find helpful as you clean up the mess and junk in your life.

Actions Of The Day

1. Take 1-2 hours today to declutter (select 1-2 items from the list identified above). P.S. Get in the habit of completely cleaning off your desk every day!

2. Select 1-2 events/groups/activities that are creating clutter in your life, and that you do not enjoy. Commit to taking at least one off of your plate by the end of this week.

# Day 2 - Define Your Vision

If you have seen the movie **'The Secret'**, you know how imperative it is to create your future. If you have not defined where you are going in clear, visual form, you are not creating and you will likely be in the same place you are today five years from now. If you are committed to building wealth and success, book two hours right now within the next 3 days; when you will sit down with yourself and a tea and create your vision. I personally have set my computer screen monitor with my dream home as a background. There are also several software programs that allow you to create your vision board online. You can have the pictures rotate throughout the day on your screen. I have three vision boards in my house; one in my office as well as two others in different locations.

A great tool for creating your vision can be found by visiting the website of **John Assaraf**. There is also a great video clip on the website about vision boards. I've gone a step further and put together my personal vision movie using Microsoft Movie Maker. Another great vision board option I use is through a wonderful site called **Mind Movies**. This allows me to watch my own vision movie every morning when I wake up. You must have a clear, definite mental picture before you can move forward with your dreams and goals. If you do not have a clear vision, then stop wasting your time and close shop immediately. The more clear and definite your mental vision is, the faster you will achieve your goals. Do you want to be on the 10-year plan or the 2-year plan? It's up to you. As of today, you are now successfully starting with the end in mind.

***"We all have two choices: We can make a living or we can design a life"***
***- Jim Rohn***

Actions Of The Day

1. Write down 50 things you want to do, have or become.

2. Begin your vision board whether online or on a poster board. Collect at least 10 pictures today that inspire you and illustrate your vision. I suggest writing out your vision first and then putting it into picture form. Think of a 2-3 year vision from today. What would you like to create for yourself? Use your list of '50 things' to create this vision.

3. Watch the movie 'The Secret' or watch it again if you already have.

# Day 3 - Your 30-Day Goal

Take fifteen to thirty minutes today in peace and silence to really get specific about what you would like to achieve by Day 30. What would you like to have, do or become? Describe in one page the specifics of this goal, describing your vision with color, texture, description, and feeling. How will you feel when you achieve this? Find a powerful picture that illustrates this goal. Post this picture on the ceiling on top of your bed. We will later discuss why this picture on your ceiling will be a helpful aid in achieving your vision. This 30-day goal can also be an excellent start to beginning a goal book. Using a sketch or scrapbook, write your 30 day goal on the first page. Again, be as specific as possible about your vision; including color, form, shape, and any other description. Make that goal have a life and identify what feelings come up for you as you write down each goal? Each page can and should have words and pictures associated with this goal. Once this 30-day program is complete, you can add some further goals to your goal book.

***"The brain is a goal-seeking organism. Whatever goal you give to your subconscious mind, it will work night and day to achieve"***

***-Jack Canfield***

We've all heard time and time again that a goal should be specific, time specific, and measurable, but more importantly, you want the goal you write down to stir something up inside of you. You want to 'feel' the feelings associated with achieving this goal. In order to achieve your goal, you must act as if that goal is already achieved.

I have found a great resource that you can use to track your goals.

During the Christmas holidays, I spend a day at my favorite coffee shop with some blank pages to help begin to brainstorm and visualize my year. I also bring my goal worksheet and begin to create my year with specific, measurable goals. A great template that I use is from Jack Canfield. He has an amazing, free **'21 Day Success Principles Mentoring Program'** on his website. After you register, you will receive the goal template as one of the bonuses for registering. You have to find what works for you!

At the end of each year, I set aside a 'creation day,' where I set my goals for the next year. This works for me. I also have my goal book that expands on each goal and helps me visualize that goal as already being achieved.

If you are looking for some coaching or tools to help you practice the art of setting and achieving goals, **Cynthia Kersey** has a great 30 Day Goal Setting program.

Actions Of The Day

1. Spend 30 minutes today decluttering your office and desk.

2. Spend 15-20 minutes flipping through a few magazines to find 2-3 more pictures for your vision board.

3. Before you go to bed, begin to craft and clarify your 30-day goal (you can begin this goal with the end already in mind). Write this goal on a small card and put the card in your wallet. Also, write this goal on a white board or large piece of paper for your office and post your goal in a spot where you can see it throughout the day. Example: On March 12, 2008, I am happy and grateful that I have successfully...

# Day 4 - Book a One Day or Personal Weekend Retreat

Today, I want you to book in your calendar, a minimum of one day within the next month, when you will take a personal wellness day. This personal wellness day is non-negotiable. This day is for you to retreat somewhere; book yourself into a luxury hotel room, B&B, retreat center or even a friend's place, to relax and unwind. Most importantly, this personal wellness day is not to be at your home, where you will be too easily distracted. Even better than a personal wellness day, would be a two-day weekend retreat!

Here are some destinations I recommend for a personal wellness day (or two): **American Yogini, Harmony Dawn, Kripalu, White Oaks Resort, St-Anne's Spa, Omega Institute, Chopra Centre**.

You'll be amazed at the ideas and creativity that come out of a one day retreat.

***"Most people who live among the crowd never press the pause button in their lives and stop for even sixty seconds to reflect on why they are here and what they are meant to do. Leadership and personal success require that we become more thoughtful than ordinary people. Stop being busy being busy. Become more reflective."***

***–Robin Sharma***

Actions Of The Day

1. Book a 1-2 day retreat in your calendar within the next 10 days. If you cannot travel far, book yourself into a hotel room or B&B for at least one night.

2. Review your vision and read your 30-day goal. Read your 30-day goal out loud and ensure that the thought of completing it excites you!

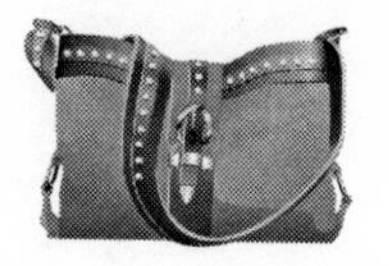

# Day 5 - An Attitude of Gratitude

With our insane schedules, it is rare that we take even a few minutes out of our day to be grateful for what we have. It really helped me to read **'The Power of Now'** by Eckhart Tolle, who speaks about how being grateful can help an individual achieve their goals. You might wonder what achieving your dreams/goals/vision has to do with Gratitude... Everything! When we are always living for tomorrow, we cannot appreciate any of the wonderful people, things and events in our life today. I can promise you, if you begin to spend more time being grateful, all kinds of wonderful things will begin to happen.

Gratitude keeps you in harmony with the laws of nature and with creativity. There is a law of gratitude and if you want results, you must recognize and observe this law. Without gratitude, you can find yourself in a cycle of being easily disappointed and dissatisfied with life. The grateful mind continues to expect incredible things. There is a great **Gratitude Journal** available from the makers of the movie 'The Secret,' to help you get started.

***"The Grateful Mind is constantly fixed upon the best"***

***- Wallace D. Wattles***

Actions Of The Day

1. Write down 20 things you are grateful for today in your life.

2. Review your vision and read your 30-day goal. Read your 30-day goal out loud and ensure that the thought of completing it excites you!

# Day 6 - Time is Money

Have a notepad handy with you throughout the day today. Every hour, document what you have done with your time. You will be surprised where your time goes. Remember, both wealthy and broke people have 24 hours in a day. Wealth builders become very conscious of how they make use of their time, and become master time-managers.

Do not forget that the 80/20 rule applies in your business as well. Tim Ferris, author of 'The 4-Hour Work Week' recommends doing an 80-20 analysis of your business and your personal life every 2-4 weeks.

Donald Trump suggests giving a monetary value to every hour of your time. He suggests acting like each hour of your time is worth $500. If you waste your time, you are losing money quickly. When you get stuck on the email for hours at a time, there goes thousands of dollars. I promise you, once you develop the skill of keeping track of what you do with your time, your income will soar. Wealthy people do the same activities as everybody else, but they do them with much more efficiency.

Actions Of The Day

1. Carry a notepad and pen in your purse/bag today. Every hour, record what activities you spent your time doing during that hour.

2. Before bed, review your notepad and see where you spent your energy. What did you spend each hour doing? Do these activities generate income or are many of them just time-wasters?

3. Before you go to sleep, read your list of the 20 things you are grateful for.

# Day 7 - Eliminate Email Insanity

Make today a no-email day. You will be surprised at how you will feel; your stress levels will be reduced, your mental state will be clearer and even your creativity will likely be heightened. How much time do you waste each day answering emails that do not result in a sale, or that can be answered with an autoresponder? As of right now, be aware of how many emails you send that are costing you unnecessary amounts of time and money.

Your email inbox is not a library. Keep your email inbox to less than one page. My rule of thumb is to keep my inbox at a level that does not reach the bottom of my screen (so I can see white space in my inbox). Also, stop checking your email as soon as you wake up in the morning. This sets the tone for your day, where not only do you have a complete lack of focus and an overwhelming amount of mental clutter, but your ability to be optimally creative and productive is jeopardized. Instead of checking your email all day long, select three specific times during the day when you can devote 20-30 minutes. During each time block, check and answer your email and get your online 'to-do's' done. End your day with mental peace and clarity as well, which means, do not be on email right before bed.

Actions Of The Day

1. Do not check your email today (I promise, you'll be ok!). Activate your autoresponder/out-of-office assistant so people know you are not returning emails today.

2. Turn your phone on silent just for today. You can check messages!

3. Before you go to sleep, read your 30-day goal and your list of the 20 things you are grateful for.

# Day 8 - Say No to the Good and YES to the Great

For many of us, we spend decades saying yes to anything and everything in fear of offending people should we say no. This is a major roadblock to building wealth. We end up being involved in so many things and events that are not aligned with where we want to be two years from now, that we completely lose focus. This includes being involved in too many networking events, too many social groups and too many boards. I watch many entrepreneurs go from networking event to networking event with the same people and one year down the road, they still are not making more money. What happened?

Saying 'no' is tough to do. Especially when we live in such a busy environment, where we work and strive to build great relationships. It is definitely a process to learn how to develop the art of saying 'no'.

Actions of the Day

1. Come up with your personal 'no' response, that you will use moving forward. Example: I wish I could but I am already fully booked/committed. If my schedule changes, I will be sure to touch base with you immediately.

2. Practice saying your 'no' response out loud 6 times throughout the day.

3. Commit to not saying 'yes' when you mean 'no'.

4. Read your 30-day goal before bed, along with your Day 5 Gratitude List.

# Day 9 - What's Your Net Worth?

We do this for our business on a regular basis. Why don't we do it for our personal finances? Even if we do create a net worth for personal finances, it is often not enough. Today, I would like you to create your personal net worth statement. If you are looking for a starting point to help guide you through evaluating your net worth, check out the Net Worth Tool at **MsMoney**.

Before you move any further, you must know your current net worth. Even if the situation is stressful or grim, you cannot improve if you do not know your starting point. Put it all on paper. Get it out in the open. During your next 30 days, you will be improving your money management skills, improving your financial literacy and financial intelligence.

Actions Of The Day

1. Create your personal net worth statement (it does not have to be a great big spreadsheet). Review your income/expenses and your assets/liabilities.

2. Before bed, review your notepad and see where you spent your energy today. What did you spend each hour doing? Do these activities generate income or are many of them time-wasters?

# Day 10 - Money Can't Talk But It Can Hear

Write down five different thoughts that frequently go through your mind when it comes to money. Be honest with yourself. What statements and phrases did your parents use repeatedly when referring to money? Some common phrases:

- I shouldn't buy that
- I can't afford it
- I need to pay off my debt
- When I pay off my debt, I will....
- Is it on sale?
- When I have more money, I will...
- I am broke

Are you focused on your current money situation or do you see yourself as already being wealthy? This is one of the key differences between the wealthy and the broke. Wealthy people 'acted' wealthy before they had money. Do you 'hold off' and 'wait' until the money comes or do you act as though you have all the money you need already. Do you focus on how much you currently have in your bank account or do you train your mind to believe you already have your $50,000 cash sitting in the bank? Remember, money is a form of energy flowing at all times. It is listening to your thoughts and your words. Stop affirming words and phrases of lack - about not having money or being broke. 'How can I afford it' should be what you think and say, instead of 'I cannot afford it'.

Actions Of The Day

1. Identify 5 common habits/affirmations that are regular thoughts/words you express when it comes to money (i.e. I'm in debt, I'm broke, I can't afford it...)

2. Replace each one of these habits/repeated affirmations with a wealthy twist, such as: 'I will be purchasing that by June 12, 2010, my money is tied up at the moment but I foresee having the funds to acquire that next month'. Find a statement that creates a sense in yourself that the money is on its way and you believe with confidence that your current situation is very temporary. Practice acting as if you have $100,000 in the bank right now.

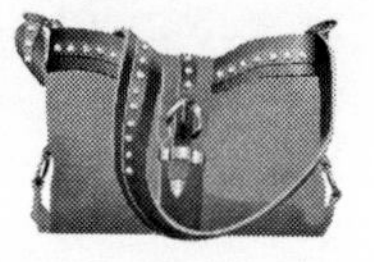

## Day 11 - Read, Think & Grow Rich

**Think and Grow Rich** by Napoleon Hill is a classic and a must. I have every version of Think and Grow Rich, the eBook, the unabridged audio, the summary audio, and continue to study the material regularly. Everyone who is incredibly successful that I've interviewed has quoted this book as being a personal favorite. This book acts as your personal mentor, and it costs less than $15; it should be referred to daily. I had the privilege of reading a copy that Bob Proctor carries around. Even today, he continues to read it daily. Buy it today and read chapter one before bed.

There are dozens of eBooks, articles and seminars out there that teach the same principles and practices that you will find in this book. I suggest buying a copy of the book but also downloading the audio version at iTunes or audible.com. This way, when you're walking, running or working out, you can become a money magnet.

In Chapter Two of 'Think and Grow Rich,' you'll read "Six Ways To Turn Desires Into Gold." Here are the main points covered in the chapter:

1) Fix in your mind the exact amount of money you desire.
2) Determine exactly what you intend to give in return for the money you desire.
3) Establish a definite plan about when you intend to possess the money you desire.
4) Create a definite plan for carrying out your desire and begin at once.

5) Write a clear, concise statement on the amount of money you intend to acquire, when you intend to acquire this money and what you will give in return for the money.

6) Read your written statement aloud twice daily; once in the morning and once before bed.

**Taken from Chapter 3 of 'Think and Grow Rich' by Napoleon Hill*

Actions Of The Day

1. Read Chapter 1 and 2 from 'Think & Grow Rich.'

2. Read your 30-day goal before bed.

3. Write out 20 things you are grateful for today.

# Day 12 - Profits are Better than Wages

For over a decade, I believed that working for wages at a great company in a great position would set me up for financial success. As I educated myself more and more on what wealthy people do, I realized that working for yourself is the only way to go. If you can work in an environment where you focus on profits and not on hourly wages, you accelerate your wealth building.

One of my favorite business philosophers and speakers is Jim Rohn. Throughout his career, he has put together several cd programs that I have found extremely valuable. One of the key lessons he teaches is profits are better than wages. I was working at a corporate job when I first heard that statement; it happened in March 2006 when I was driving to the airport to pick up my boss. I had never heard this statement before, and while a part of me felt disappointed that I was working for wages, I was inspired and excited to begin my journey to working for profits!! Within 7 months, I quit my job and was working for profits! Thank you Jim Rohn. If you would like to listen to the cd program I first stumbled upon by Jim Rohn, it is called **The Challenge to Succeed**.

Actions Of The Day

1. Turn your car/commuting time into a university class. Select 1-2 books from our reference list. Challenge to Succeed is available as an mp3. iTunes carries most of the books in our reference list, and you can download the mp3 versions of the books from iTunes.

2. Read your 30-day goal before bed.

3. Read one Chapter from 'Think & Grow Rich.'

# Day 13 - In Love With Leverage

Leverage means doing more with less. Working smarter instead of harder is what leverage creates. This is not easy to do as we have been trained and programmed to work hard for money. As T. Harv Eker would say "If you're not using leverage, you're working too hard, and earning too little."

Leverage is using other people's talents, time, skills, contacts, credibility, money and resources.

***A Life Without Leverage***

Before the age of 29, I had never heard about the concept of leverage. Granted, I never took the time to learn more about how wealthy people lived before that age, but I do not recall anyone from any of my educational institutions who provided me with this crucial information. Up until the age of 29, I spent every hour of everyday working as hard as I could and as fast as I could from morning until night. I often wondered why my vacations were spent crashing and just wanting to tune out and turn off for a full week. I would work all day, workout over my lunch hour, go to school at night and try to do every single activity with excellence - ALL BY MYSELF. The competitive work and school environments would simply accelerate this internal drive to do everything myself as 'perfectly' as possible. So why was it that as I moved up the corporate ladder as quickly as I could, and completed my MBA as fast as I could, I was no closer to being wealthy than I was five years prior to joining the workforce and starting and completing my MBA? I could not possibly do more or be more…or could I?

As I mentioned before, at the age of 29, the magical formula was finally introduced to me. By working less, but working more strategically and purposefully, I could earn more, increase my energy and produce more. The solution to my problem was LEVERAGE. All I needed to do was to shift my mindset. I needed to learn that I was working backwards. Doing everything myself was actually keeping me from becoming wealthy. Who knew? It took me another year to practice leverage and to break my old habits. In theory, it sounds great - delegate, focus on what you are great at and leverage the knowledge, money and expertise of other people. In practice, this goes against anything and everything we have been taught in school and in life. It takes some de-programming and some practice to build the momentum associated with leverage.

***"I would rather have 1% of the efforts of 100 people than 100% of my own efforts."***
***-J. Paul Getty***

Actions Of The Day

1. If you removed yourself from your business, would you still have streams of income? Would your business continue to thrive? Do you have leverage?

2. What is the first area where you will begin implementing leverage in your business as of today?

- Other People's companies/ Money (sponsorships/ funding)
- Other People's Time (free up your time)
- Other People's Resources (seek out people with expertise)
- Power of The Media (leverage the media for events/ brands/projects)
- Power of Technology (virtual assistants, autoresponders, time-savers)
- Other people's contacts (tap into other people's networks)

3. Read one chapter from 'Think and Grow Rich.'

# Day 14 - Seek a Millionaire Mentor

Notice I said 'Millionaire Mentor'. I often see individuals seeking coaching from people or businesses that are basically at the same financial and state of success as they are. If you want to accelerate your growth, you need to learn from people who are already there and will bring you up a notch. It is like hiring a personal trainer who is in the same shape as you. Where will your inspiration come from? These millionaire mentors are not easy to find, but if you jump out of your comfort zone and actively seek these mentors, you can do it. I have been able to do this year after year with no previous contacts or referrals. I simply selected my 'dream mentors' and contacted them or their company. I challenge you to identify 3-4 millionaires, or very successful people you admire and get in touch with them. Pick up the phone! If they cannot help you, they will most definitely point you in the right direction. What is the worst that can happen? I'll tell you…they are too busy to act as your mentor but I emphasize this point, they will most definitely point you in the direction of someone they would recommend for you. My challenge for you today is to pick 3-4 individuals and go for it. Pick up the phone; email them or their company… ASK!!!

I am an advocate of mentorship and mentoring programs. Having a great mentor to learn from and be accountable to is an incredible way to accelerate your learning process and your business. Although I do not have a formal coaching business, I do have a personal passion for mentoring women in business. Find someone you admire and seek out a mentor.

If you do not currently have a mentor, you can hire one virtually!

**The Science of Getting Rich** by Bob Proctor, Jack Canfield and Dr. Michael Beckwith is a fantastic program I came across earlier this year and continue to study.

Actions Of The Day

1. Identify 10 individuals who are successful both financially and in their personal life that you would love to have as a mentor.

2. Commit to contacting at least 5 of them within the next 24-48 hours.

3. Read one Chapter from 'Think & Grow Rich.'

4. Read your 30-day goal before bed.

# Day 15 - Build Million Dollar Relationships / Circle of Influence

Networking is one of the great skills of building any business. You've likely heard the saying 'If you're not networking, you're not working'. It takes practice to become a master networker, but one of the key principles to being a great networker is being of incredible service to others. Have you ever been to a networking event and dozens of people throw their business cards in your face? I'm not sure if anyone told those people that they are throwing away money by being more interested in themselves than in others. Check out our **<u>'Top 10 Tips for Networking with Excellence'</u>** article.

Once you begin to develop your networking skills (some of you are likely already experts), you will want to begin to network with individuals who have achieved your personal goal. You are not likely to find them among your current circle of friends. If you have seen the movie 'The Secret,' they explain how your current income is an average of your five closest friends, and how we tend to surround ourselves with individuals who are at similar income levels. In order to accelerate your wealth and business building, you are going to want to seek out a million dollar circle of influence.

***<u>The Secret Friends</u>***

Two "Million Dollar Relationships" that are very significant to me are the ones I initiated with **Bob Proctor** and **Loral Langemeier**. Both of these individuals have had a tremendous impact on my life. After attending their seminars and becoming involved in their coaching programs, I was able to establish communication with both Loral Langemeier and Bob Proctor. Within 8 months, Loral agreed to fly to Toronto in March 2008 to act as a keynote speaker for my very first event **WellSpot 2008**. Loral is one of the most incredible speakers I have seen and I could not have imagined I would be spending time with her at my very own event. I also had the pleasure of spending time with Bob Proctor, whom I have admired and respected for years. I had seen him speak several times and had read his book **'You Were Born Rich'** one year earlier. I had the pleasure of listening to him discuss his favorite books, his company and his personal philosophy.

**Your Circle of Influence**

As I mentioned earlier, your income is an average of your five closest friends. That was a shocker to me when I first heard it! It did not take me long to start meeting new friends after I became aware of this fact. Today, I challenge you to book a coffee/lunch with three individuals who are successful leaders that you admire and would like in your circle of friends.

Facebook is a fantastic tool for getting in touch with some of those incredible millionaire mentors. I make sure I add my favorite authors, speakers, coaches and thriving entrepreneurs to my Facebook network. It is a great way to get in touch with them and join any groups they have going on, so you can keep up with their events, seminars, books and any other sources they recommend.

You want to surround yourself with people who have inspiring visions. Is there anyone in your life who is bringing you down? Is there anyone in your life that may be toxic and detrimental to you as you create your vision?

Actions Of The Day

1. Take 45 minutes today to brainstorm about an organization, charity, board of directors or group that you want in your new circle of influence. I challenge you to jump 'up' and out of your comfort zone. You want to surround yourself with wealthy, successful entrepreneurs who you can learn from. Commit yourself to establishing contact with two entrepreneurs from your list. Research which one is the best fit for you and your business.

2. Review your current networking groups/events and identify if the networks you associate yourself with are all at the same level as you are. I challenge you to change this. I am not saying drop networking groups and events that involve your current circle of influence and friends, but look at how often and how much time they consume. Perhaps you could remove one and add a new 'Million Dollar Circle of Influence.'

3. Read your list of - '20 Things I am Grateful For' from Day 5.

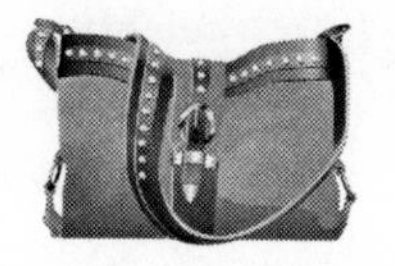

# Day 16 - Multiple Streams of Income

Focus on making your Multiple Streams of Income passive. This means they require little maintenance or management from you personally. In the 1950's, it only took one stream of income for a family to survive. Today, it takes at least two streams of income for a family to survive. In the future, people will need a portfolio of income streams from many different and diversified sources. In this optimal situation, if one stream goes, you do not give it much notice. You are stable. You have time to adjust.

Prosperous people have always known this. If one stream dries up for them, they have many more streams to support them. Most people are much more vulnerable. If they lose one of their streams, it wipes them out financially. And it takes them years to recover. There are great resources for you to further explore and educate yourself on multiple income streams, such as Multiple Streams of Income with Robert Allen. You can also contact me to discuss some other great resources.

We will review in further detail some ideas for initiating multiple streams of income. Some of the more common ones include:

- Rental Properties (generating positive cash flow)
- Online Affiliate Programs
- Investments
- Direct Selling/Network Marketing
- Products (eBooks, books, product lines, audio programs)

***Note About Affiliate Programs***

I do want to emphasize that affiliate programs are a simple way to begin adding an additional stream of income to your business.
It takes a great deal of effort to learn how to work affiliate programs

properly, but they can potentially bring you some great passive monthly and even passive weekly income. I would suggest that you do your homework and spend some time learning about how affiliate programs work. Some of your favorite products may have online affiliate programs, where you can earn commission by recommending these products online. A few great affiliate program resources include **AffiliateProgram.com** and **Affiliate Tips**. Do not get discouraged if it takes you some time to make money; you will need to practice, experiment and run some trial and error tests.

Make a checklist of 20 of your favorite speakers, coaches, authors, products and websites. It is possible that they have affiliate programs that you can register to be a part of and earn a commission for recommending their products/services. Usually, they will have a link called 'affiliates' on their website.

Actions Of The Day

1. Make your list of 20 of your favorite products, speakers, websites and authors and check their websites to see if they have an affiliate program. Select 3-5 affiliate programs you want to register to.

2. Put your affiliate information (passwords and login) in a safe place until day 25.

3. Begin to research, brainstorm and identify your next income stream for your future MSI portfolio. Affiliate programs are a great start, and it will only take you a few minutes to get connected! All you need is a site, blog, or database, where you can post and share links. A Millionaire Mentor is also a great person to ask for input and advice!

4. Review your vision and read your 30-day goal before bed.

# Day 17 - Get on the Road to Residual

Building on our Day 16 principle of MSI's, I want to clarify that what you really want is multiple streams of residual income. Residual income is an income stream that is not dependant on your time and personal energy. Residual income streams are a must to building sustainable wealth. Residual income streams flow steadily and allow the efforts you put out today to pay off multiple times. Residual income streams last a lifetime and beyond.

There are three common ways to build a residual income.

1) Real Estate (takes up to 27 yrs).
2) Savings & Investing (takes up to 23 years).
3) Network Marketing (takes 3-4 years).

Three years ago, I became very aware that I had no streams of residual income. I did have a rental property, but it was not generating positive cash flow each month. I did not have the extra income required to invest, and I was not ready to add another source of income to my portfolio. The third option was getting involved in network marketing. I was not very familiar with network marketing and had no experience in direct sales. Being open minded and interested in being financially free by 35, I figured I had to at least do some investigating. I selected a company from over 2000 in the industry that I felt best suited me and was best in its class. From there, I spoke to individuals who were making a significant amount of income, and from them, I learned how to be successful. I decided that if Robert Allen, Robert Kiyosaki, Paul Zane Pelzer, Donald Trump, Warren Buffet, Steven Covey and so many other millionaires were recommending the network marketing industry, I would listen to the experts. Three years later, I successfully generated a six-figure residual income stream from an industry that is still in its infancy. Wait five years and watch how many people you know become involved in this industry. It is not for everyone, but there are many positive aspects about the industry. I like the following:

1) You set your own hours.
2) You work from home.
3) You work with people you like.
4) You learn the true meaning of teamwork.
5) You can generate a 40-year income in 3 years.
6) You learn how to become an excellent money manager.
7) You learn the true power of Leverage.
8) If you are still in a job you dislike, you can fire your boss within a year.

***"One-to-one marketing is already a force to be reckoned with—but there is an explosion ahead".*** ***– Paul Zane Pilzer***

Actions Of The Day

1. Answer the following questions:
   Do you currently have an income stream that works 24-7, even while you sleep?
   Do you have more than one consistent income stream?
   Do you experience >10% growth year after year?

   If the answer is no to these three questions, take 30 minutes today to research, and brainstorm on paper some possible residual streams of income that fit with your personal interests and skills. Ask 3-4 financially successful friends/associates if they have residual streams of income and what these residual streams of income are.

2. Read one chapter from 'Think & Grow Rich' before bed.

3. Review your vision and read your 30-day goal before bed.

# Day 18 - Create Cash Flow

Here's where most people get into financial trouble. If you cannot manage cash flow, you will never build wealth. If you are focused on paying off your debt (even if it means having a negative cash flow), today is your day to take this on. Take control of your cash flow!

I recently came across the book and website for 'Smart Cookies.' The reason I like it is because the founders of 'Smart Cookies' simplify and add an element of fun to their discussion of money management. Their website has a great section for downloads, where you can find a few money management templates that work for you. The 'Smart Cookies' website has a great budget sheet and spending snapshot. Another great website which gives excellent budgeting and financial advice is **Geezeo**.

***Cash Flow Producing Assets***

Most people lack cash flow producing assets. I will not discuss this topic in detail, but it is highly recommended that you investigate and evaluate opportunities for increasing cash flow through these types of assets. For example, invest in real estate that you can rent out that creates a monthly cash flow. I had a great learning experience a few years back. I was getting into the home rental market but I was only able to cover my expenses each month. I quickly realized that other than some appreciation, I did not have any cash flow producing assets. I therefore decided to sell my home, which turned out to be the best decision I could have made. I made a 40% return within two years of purchasing the home.

How long could you live without going into debt if your income stopped tomorrow?
Most people could barely survive past one week without going into serious debt. Commit yourself today to becoming an excellent money manager! It does not happen overnight.

Here are some steps I took to become a capable and competent money manager:

1) I read books (check out the reference guide at the end).
2) I hired a bookkeeper.
3) I hired a 'Million Dollar Financial Planner.'
4) I learned how to properly manage and distribute my paychecks (between paying off debts, putting money in my savings account, giving money to charity, and investing).

Actions Of The Day

1. Download the spending snapshot from the Smart Cookies site (link is above). Fill out your spending/ cash flow needs per month. Review your current cash flow situation (is it negative?).

2. Write down 20 ways you could increase your cash flow by $200 per month (write an eBook, run a seminar, join/support affiliate programs).

3. As of today, commit yourself to the process of learning and practicing the techniques and habits required of an excellent money manager.

4. Read one Chapter from 'Think & Grow Rich' before bed.

# Day 19 - Set Your Financial Freedom Day

My financial freedom day is September 12, 2010! I thought it would be valuable to share my personal date with you all; a date that I set when I was still working in a corporate environment. Even back then, I knew that if I stayed where I was (working for wages), and continued to walk the path I was walking, I knew that becoming financially free by 35 years old would be impossible.

When I first set my financial freedom date as September 12, 2010, many people laughed at my goal. I did not let that distract me from keeping my focus on achieving this goal. For those people who did not show the same confidence and enthusiasm in my goal as I did, I just told them to expect a postcard from me on that day. I do believe that you have to set a financial freedom date for yourself that is somewhat believable for you. If you set your financial freedom date for six months from now, and you are $100,000 in debt, this goal is not going to stir up any excitement, or feelings of hope and anticipation. More likely, it will create great stress and chaos in your life, as you will not believe it is even possible. I selected a date that was three years away but I have met people who have selected a date one year in the future and have achieved financial freedom - so it is possible. The most important thing to do once this date is set is to surround yourself with the best people, coaches, financial partners and of course, to prepare a good, solid plan of action.

***Create A Wealth Account***

**Loral Langemeier** discusses the concept of the 'wealth account' in her book 'The Millionaire Maker' in further detail. The major problem today with insane credit card debt is that most people spend much more than they earn. Also, people are putting their money in savings accounts with very low returns, in the hope of having enough by the time they retire to live their 'Golden Years' in financial freedom. The reality is that only 1 in 100 people will be wealthy by the age of their retirement.

Open a 'Wealth Account' even if you are generating little interest, you can use this account to accumulate money that you will use to invest in cash flow generating assets. I recommend you have a certain amount of money automatically withdrawn from your main account each pay period, and transferred into your Wealth Account. This wealth account will be used to build new streams of passive income (such as investing in real estate, business ventures, etc). The money in this 'Wealth Account' account will be used to work for you!

Get rid of bad debt! Bad debt is debt that you are paying off yourself with your blood, sweat and tears. Those credit cards are a great place to begin. Robert Kiyosaki has some great suggestions about getting rid of bad debt in his book 'Guide to Becoming Rich.' Here are some of his suggestions:

1) Get rid of all credit cards except for 1 or 2.
2) As of today, any new charges that you add to the 1 or 2 remaining cards must be paid off every month. Do not incur any further long-term debts.
3) Pay off monthly minimums on both cards.
4) Come up with $150-$200 extra per month (generate more income!)
5) Apply this additional $150-$200 per month to your monthly payment of one of your credit cards. Pay only the minimum on the other card.
6) Once one card is paid off, apply the same amount of money to the next card, in addition to that card's monthly payment. Note: you are now paying the monthly minimum plus the total monthly payment from the first credit card.

7) When the credit cards are paid off, continue this process with your car and home payments.
8) When you are debt free, take the monthly payment amount and put that money towards investments and building your assets.

Negotiate a better interest rate on your cards with your banking institution!

Actions Of The Day

1. Take 15 minutes before you go to sleep tonight and set your Financial Freedom Date. Mark your calendar, your day planner, your blackberry. Mark this date in several places, and especially mark this date in a visible place where you can see it daily. Also, set a clear monetary value for what financially free means to you. Is it $30,000 per month or $30,000 per week? What will you do with this money, and what will you give in return for receiving this money?

2. Read two Chapters from 'Think and Grow Rich.'

3. Read your 30-day goal before bed.

# Day 20 - Wealth Begins In The Mind

One of the best books around on understanding the mind's role in creating the lifestyle you want is **'The Power of the Subconscious Mind'** by Dr. Joseph Murphy. I suggest reading it more than once. There are so many great insights and stories in this book. It is more like a reference book! Just read it!

Your subconscious mind operates in an orderly manner and expresses itself through your feelings and thoughts. Over the past two years, a very big part of my reading and practice has been in the area of the subconscious mind. Our behavior, habits, and life results are programmed by our subconscious mind. Dr. Joseph Murphy explains that what you write and repeatedly say to yourself on the inside will be your experience on the outside.

Repeat the word 'success' to yourself frequently with confidence, and you will be under a subconscious compulsion to succeed and achieve.

***Weird Coincidence?***

From the age of 17 or 18, I often had recurring dreams about a man in my life that was tall (over 6 feet), had dark hair, light eyes and was French. I know it sounds like that handsome prince we all dream about, but this was different. I vividly remember a dream I would frequently have about this man, but had no idea who he was. Not familiar with the lessons that I am writing about today, I had no conscious idea about techniques such a visualization, psycho-pictography or training your subconscious mind through imagery. I continued on for many years not quite making out what this dream was communicating to me. At the age of 24, I was married to a wonderful man. I did not think much of this dream of course, but would occasionally continue to dream that same dream from years ago. My husband was not French; he had blonde hair and blue eyes and was my best friend. I figured that dream of mine was some bizarre memory from when I was a child attending French school, and so, I continued to shrug it off.

By 28, my marriage was ending. Although we had a wonderful friendship, we maturely decided our relationship was not destined for a long-term future and a family. We parted ways and I became a 28-year-old divorcee. I remember being at a bar one evening shortly after my divorce was final and thinking that I must be the youngest divorcee at the bar. That title made me cringe! Most of my friends were just beginning their marriages, and here I was, young and divorced.

As difficult as it was, this was one of the best times of my life. I had to face some of my greatest fears and learn to truly believe that there was a bigger plan for me in this world. I had faith that something wonderful was in my future, and it was my duty to continue on my journey to self-discovery and personal growth.

Two jobs, one three month trip to Europe and 12 cities later, I found myself back in my hometown of Burlington, Ontario. I was back living with my parents, and this was a nice comforting time. I had just started a new job as a sales manager in Toronto. But, here is where things get 'creepy'.

Not only was I now traveling to Montreal almost weekly for my new job, I was getting phone calls from a wonderful friend from my former workplace about a wonderful man she wanted me to meet. She asked me if I would be open to an informal lunch with her, and she would bring him along. That way, should I not be interested, we could pass it off as a friendly lunch. I agreed.

As I approached our neutral Starbucks meeting place, I saw my friend Emily approach. I assumed the guy she was with was 'him'. He was incredibly cute I thought to myself, and with a bizarre internal nudge, I felt as if I already knew him. He was 6'2 with dark hair, green eyes and a French accent. No word of a lie... it was the guy from my dreams.

Christian and I now live together at our home in Burlington, and we have been together for four years. We have built an incredible relationship together, and are both very aware of how mental images create reality. When I told Christian this story, he thought it was cute but I know that it was much more than that.

Exercise - Before you go to bed and first thing in the morning. What mental images do you see?

***"Your subconscious mind is your power center. It functions in every cell of your body." - Bob Proctor***

Actions Of The Day

1. Become aware of what you watch and read before you go to bed and when you wake up in the morning.

2. Purchase the book The Power of Your Subconscious Mind (or download it from iTunes).

3. Read one Chapter of 'Think and Grow Rich.'

4. Read your 30-day goal before bed.

# Day 21 - Stick - Em Up

I have a $10,000 bill on the ceiling on top of my bed, so that every night before I go to sleep, I focus on my daily residual income. I also suggest putting up sticky notes on your bathroom mirrors, as they are the first thing you see when you wake up in the morning, and the last thing you see before you go to bed. As I began this journey, the sticky notes in my bathroom said, "I am so happy and grateful now that I earn $20,000 per month." Remember that this was based on a perfectly flexible schedule - working 15 hours per week and dedicating almost two hours per day to fitness and triathlon training. In my eyes, this is true balance.

P.S. You should be getting well into **'Think and Grow Rich'** by now. You will learn that one of the secrets to this book is writing down your goal and reading it every day. You need to project this goal onto your mind as often as possible.

Actions Of The Day

1. Purchase some fun and colourful post-it notes.

2. Write down how much you will be earning per month by your financial freedom day, and write it out on your post-it note (along with your financial freedom date). Complete and post a post-it note for every bathroom mirror in your house.

3. Read one Chapter of 'Think and Grow Rich.'

4. Read your 30-day goal.

5. On the ceiling of your bedroom, stick a picture that illustrates something you want to have, be or do (i.e. your dream car, house, a fitness goal…)

# Day 22 - Define Your Personal Philosophy

Never discuss the possibility of failure or discuss ways you will deal with potential failure. Are you committed to excuses or results? Stop feeling disappointed. Hang out with professional athletes and wealthy entrepreneurs and observe how they speak and what they speak about. I guarantee they speak about Discipline, Commitment, Focus, Persistence and Winning, instead of failure and disappointment.

Have you taken the time to clearly identify your personal values and what inspires you? Do you really know what you are passionate about? Is your business aligned with your personal philosophy? For example, if one of your personal values is health and fitness, and you are working in an industry that manufactures products that contribute to chronic degenerative disease, it is going to be tough for you to create true wealth and fulfillment.

***My Personal Philosophy***

Three of my personal values are health/wellness, mentoring others and entrepreneurship. As I stated earlier, I have made a commitment to build wealth for myself by the age of 35. The reason behind this is that when I get my finances taken care of for life, I can create more incredible things for myself and for others. I can mentor and coach others with excellence, and truly embrace the power of entrepreneurship. If you can take care of building wealth for yourself now, you will be empowered to create so much more for yourself and others. I have also made it my daily practice to incorporate activities that promote optimal health, such as drinking lots of water, taking top rated multivitamins, low-glycemic eating, and incorporating a solid fitness regime and yoga into my lifestyle. I know that when I am not feeling my best, it is only because I have been working too hard and neglecting my own health.

I have made a commitment to myself, that I will surround myself daily with successful and inspiring individuals who challenge me (in a positive way), support me, and lift me up! I have absolutely no time for 'can't', 'won't', and 'impossible'. You will find if you surround yourself with the right people, those words are just not part of any conversation.

***"You can have everything in life you want, if you will just help other people get what they want"*** ***-Zig Ziglar***

Actions of the Day

1. Write down what you value the most.
2. Write down ideas and concepts that you would like to include in your personal philosophy.
3. Read one chapter of 'Think and Grow Rich.'
4. Read your 30-day goal.

# Day 23 - Just Do It

Stop waiting for a change in the environment or for circumstances to be 'just right' before you act. Leaders and wealthy entrepreneurs act before they are ready. Stop being a perfectionist. You cannot do and be everything. This is costing you thousands, if not millions of dollars.

Do things that make you nervous. Do things that you do not think you can do. Do things you are scared to do. There is never a perfect time to do anything.

***The Creation of WellSpot***

A year and a half ago, I had the bright idea of creating a big event for women in downtown Toronto about wealth and wellness. I had never organized an event before in my life (other than a few corporate sales meetings and weddings). I wanted to bring together my favorite mentors, speakers and authors, and create an annual symposium, which I called WellSpot. I put a wish list together of speakers, venues, guests, décor and everything that I wanted to include in this event. Even better, I decided to launch the event within six months!

The event turned out to be an incredible success. We had 270 guests in attendance, over 12 sponsors and an incredible line-up of speakers including: Olympic Gold Medalist **Jennifer Azzi**, financial expert and best-selling author **Loral Langemeier**, top author and raw food expert **Kimberly Mac**, Canadian songstress **Sarah Slean**, best-selling author of 'The Eat Clean Diet' **Tosca Reno**, speaker and career coach **Tama Kieves**, as well as spiritual teachers **Matt Kahn** and **Julie Dittmar**. We received great media coverage, and are currently beginning early stage planning for our next **WellSpot** event in 2010.

Even with the poor planning, poor budgeting, a lack of knowledge about event planning, and absolutely no idea about how to pull it off, we managed to create an incredible first year event. Thanks to three incredible individuals (Michelle Froats, Sarah Webb and Christian Dion), along with a beautiful team of volunteers, the day was an incredible success. My motto, perhaps learned from Nike, is 'just do it'. Sure it could have been planned better but I will leave the refining and perfecting of the event for year number two. My key advice for those of you who want to put on large events:

1) Put together a superstar team from day one.
2) Recruit some great interns (event and PR students are super!)
3) Over-estimate the expenses on your budget.
4) Delegate, Delegate, Delegate!
5) Take extra good care of yourself. You will need a health program during this time!!! Massages, a solid fitness regime, follow a great nutrition program, and take a great vitamin!!!
6) Just book a date for the event, and work backwards from there.
7) Do not wait until you feel ready. Jump out of your comfort zone.
8) Put together a PR campaign and get a team involved to help you out.
9) Leverage social media and the Internet to advertise your event.

***<u>And a few personal learnings:</u>***

1) I will not stuff 500 goodie bags all by myself again. (Thanks Mom and Christian!!)
2) I will not overpromise.

3) I will not store stock and products in my garage for my speakers.
4) I will Invest in professional tech guys and an A/V company.
5) I will Set clear expectations with everyone involved from day one.
6) I will Plan one year out. Sponsors need lots of lead time!
7) I will Create contracts for speakers.
8) I will Leverage this event to generate post-event products/ books/ DVDs.
9) I will Hire a great team of ambassadors and affiliates to help promote the event.
10) I will Enjoy the ride! Sure, I will be stressed and overworked, but I will want to do it again!!

***"Action is the real measure of intelligence"*** ***-Napoleon Hill***

<u>Actions Of The Day</u>

1. Identify 1-2 projects you have been procrastinating about (i.e. creating a website, book, blog, event, business, or product)

2. Select a completion date TODAY for these 1-2 projects, and mark your calendar with this or these dates now.

3. Ask a friend or colleague to be your accountability coach, and share your deadline with them. Ask them to check in once a week via phone to keep you on track.

4. Read one chapter of 'Think & Grow Rich.'

5. Read your 30-day goal before bed.

# Day 24 - Create a Personal Brand & Build a Tribe

With the explosion of social media, creating your personal brand has become critical to business success, both online and off. Many women I know have been thinking of creating a business and a brand but are not really sure what to do and how to do it. Your personal brand is really how other people see you. A personal brand is formed through repeated contact. Your personal brand should be a reflection of who you are and what you love. What are you great at? What do you love to do? What would you do even if you were not paid for it? These questions should guide you in the direction of where an incredible personal brand is budding. Those who have a personal brand have done a superb job of leveraging social media. So, for those of you who are thinking about launching a brand, or you want to take your existing brand to the next level, here are a few suggestions that will help:

- Take inventory of your personal values.
- Identify your key areas of personal interest and passion.
- Take a day or two to create. Get quiet. Brainstorm. Journal. Let inspiration take over.
- Play around with drawings and paint a mental picture of what your brand could look like and be.
- Ask for help. Brainstorm with a marketing expert. Ask friends for input.
- See your brand as a super success that receives international recognition.
- Get emotional about your brand. Even if it is not created yet, start seeing it as alive and flourishing.
- Seek out expert graphic and marketing assistance at Elance

(they offer great prices!)

- Print business cards. There is nothing that says 'I'm in business' like a business card (VistaPrint or Moo).
- Learn about social media. Read lots. Attend an event on how to build a brand online. Check out Four Hour Work Week for great information and observe a great brand in action.

***A few things to keep in mind if your brand has already been launched:***

1) Be consistent.
2) Share resources. Give things away. Be generous with your knowledge.
3) Connect often.

***Build a Brand/Build a Tribe***

Some of you have likely heard of **CrossFit**. This fitness franchise is for fitness enthusiasts who like a hard core competitive workout that will leave you sweating buckets. The brand has exploded and CrossFit locations can be found across Canada, the US, as well as internationally. CrossFit has built a tribe of fitness enthusiasts who crave this unique workout and cannot get enough. The founder of CrossFit (Greg Glassman) understands how to lead a tribe. Franchise owners, members and fitness enthusiasts all work in synergy to promote the tribe, and the growth of the tribe is viral in nature. Check out the book **Tribes** by Seth Godin.

**Start a Blog**

Look at most authors, speakers and experts in any field; they all have a blog. Check out **WordPress** and **Blogger** for some suggestions about how to create a blog.
You can contact **eblink Marketing** for some great advice and input about how and where to begin (they did our **www.healthygirl.net** site).

Here are some key points to keep in mind when starting or working on improving your blog:

1) Get your domain name (**Go Daddy** or **Domains in Seconds**).
2) Install plug-ins such as a poll.
3) Host a contest to generate comments from your readers.
4) Encourage bloggers to link their blog to your blog, and encourage them to link their blog to other blogs.
5) Use eye catching photos (**www.sxc.hu**)
6) Make your blog look like a mini-magazine: include pictures and videos!
7) Offer a full feed RSS.
8) Post 2-3 entries per day.

Check out other free online resources and articles at **Ladies Who Launch** and **Problogger**.

Actions Of The Day

1. Take 30 minutes of absolute quiet, uninterrupted time today (have a bubble bath, run, walk, sit down). No distractions! Imagine your brand is featured on Oprah. What does it look like? Who does your brand appeal to? Visualize what your brand is all about.

2. Read 1 Chapter of 'Think & Grow Rich.'

3. Read your 30-day goal before bed and check out your vision board.

# Day 25 - Write an eBook / Build on Your Brand

It sounds simple, and you might think everyone is jumping on the eBook bandwagon these days, but it is more complex than you think. Writing an eBook sounds so much easier than writing a book doesn't it? Over the past year, I have learned that there is a serious science to writing eBooks. Although it takes time and efficiency, I highly recommend everyone have an eBook (and eventually a book!). Some of the great reasons to write an eBook include the following: promoting a product or blog, making money online or simply boosting your profile. If you are new to the world of online marketing, I would highly recommend you circulate your eBook free of charge and promote it everywhere and anywhere online. Here are a few key tips to writing an eBook:

1) eBook length should be between 15,000 and 30,000 words.
2) Take the time to create a really great title.
3) Set a deadline for your eBook before your even start.
4) Have it edited by a professional.
5) Make banners for online promotion of your eBook.
6) Write a sales page to promote your eBook.
7) Create pre-launch buzz (i.e. a contest, PR release, etc.).
8) If you are selling your book, create an affiliate program.
9) Ask for reviews from your first few readers.
10) If you are selling your eBook, do not forget about **lulu** and **amazon**.

Darren Rowse of Problogger has written a great article for creating an eBook.

If you are looking to make your eBook incredibly professional looking, and need some online promo tools for your book (such as graphics, banners, a microsite, cover page), I highly recommend contacting Wendy at **Get eCovers**.

Actions Of The Day

1. What three topics would you love to write a book/eBook about?

2. Read Darren Rowse's creating an eBook report.

3. What other products/services would help you build your brand and strengthen your tribe? (i.e. coaching, holding events, blogging, networking)

4. Read one chapter of 'Think & Grow Rich.'

5. Read your 30-day goal before bed.

# Day 26 - Learn How To Get Great PR

I'm definitely not a PR expert, but I have educated myself about PR through hosting my own events. You are the most incredible and passionate PR machine for your own brand. You simply need to put in some effort and be persistent! By reading newspapers and getting familiar with reports, hot topics and what companies are looking for, you can often manage to get yourself some PR coverage. Do not be shy. Contact reporters and build relationships with them. If there are some products and brands that you use regularly, contact the companies and find the Director or VP of these brands. Seek out individuals in companies who are in influential positions and have decision-making power. Share how your brand/company can help them reach their target market, and share the value of your 'tribe'. Once you create a brand and build a tribe, you will have created a beautiful network of like-minded individuals who trust the information you provide. Word of mouth marketing is an area that companies are trying to leverage. Here are a few suggestions:

- Get familiar with some of the top reporters in newspapers/ magazines that often write about topics you/your company specializes in.
- Contact decision-makers at companies that you feel are a great fit with you and your company for sponsorship/ promotion/ partnerships.
- Interview a top PR agent/publicist for some key insights.
- Make your own buzz. You are responsible for your brand and your success. Do not be afraid to toot your own horn. Create your own buzz by leveraging media and expand your database by including key people of influence in the community.

- Interview successful entrepreneurs and ask them for advice on how they generate PR.
- Leverage databases and the contacts of major companies. If you are able to team up with a company that suits your business, and your clients, often you can come up with great projects/events where you can leverage their network of employees and/or clients.
- Check out some conference calls and educational information and tools provided by Steve Harrison. He often runs free conference calls and events to help entrepreneurs generate PR.
- Join Facebook Groups and create a Facebook group for your brand/company. Leverage social media for your PR (i.e. LinkedIn/Twitter/Facebook/Myspace).
- Research further ways to generate PR. A few suggested websites include: PR Leads, PR Web, Expert Click, Newswire.
- Hire a PR Intern.
- Hire a publicist (it is worth investing in!)
- Find out what other entrepreneurs are doing! Leverage other people! Exchange value and information with each other.

Actions Of The Day

1. What would you use PR for (your brand, event, book, promoting you)?

2. Set up an interview with a successful entrepreneur to find out about their PR activities and key insights.

3. Set up an interview/coffee with a publicist or PR specialist to learn more about leveraging PR, and some easy activities you can do.

4. Read your 30-day goal.

# Day 27 - Leverage Other People's Money

There is a woman named Jen who owns a kids' clothing company. What is unique about her company is that all her fabrics are made from bamboo fibers. Once she developed, designed and manufactured her line of clothing, she had no budget left for much promotion. Jen's friend Sue owned a PR firm, and highly recommended she get on some of the top TV shows for moms, as well as the morning news shows in the US. The problem was that Jen was out of money. She could not afford a publicist or a PR blitz unless she put in the time and energy to do it herself. Sue had a great suggestion to help Jen with her money problem. "Why don't you recruit 1-2 sponsors for your clothing launch, which will pay for your PR campaign? It's a win-win! They will get exposure on all the media outlets and on your website. You'll have the financing to maximize exposure for your new incredible brand."

Whether it is a startup, an event, a book launch or a business project, it is often worth recruiting sponsors to assist in funding these activities. Remember the key word - LEVERAGE. You want to leverage your money and make good use of other people's capital that can also benefit from what you are doing.

## Actions Of The Day

1. Think of a project, event or product where you could leverage a company to help fund the product. Think of a great product that compliments what you are doing and is reaching the same target market that you want to reach.

2. Take 30 minutes today to go through your network (Facebook, Linked-in, business cards, email addresses, Outlook). Identify 7-10 possible companies that are a great fit for your brand/business that you have a contact name and information for. Initiate contact and start networking!

3. Set up an interview/coffee with one of your target companies to share ideas about how you could help them via your brand.

4. Read your 30-day goal.

# Day 28 - The Bookkeeper, Housecleaner And Virtual Assistant

As Robert Kiyosaki says, you did not go into business to learn how to be a bookkeeper, so delegate what you can and focus on earning money!

Three key ingredients on the road to wealth:

***Your Bookkeeper***

Being an excellent money manager is absolutely crucial to building wealth. You may have the skills and the time to do your own books, record all your receipts and evaluate where you spend your money, but should you? Imagine the income you could generate if you took this time and spent it engaging in activities you are great at. Let's take a six hour window for example. Say you had a professional build you a spreadsheet, enter your receipts and provide you with a full analysis of your monthly monetary transactions. During that same period of time, you successfully booked three new clients and partnered with one new corporate sponsor who is willing to completely fund the launch of your first book. That is the magic of hiring someone who 'plays at what you work at,' meaning they do it with more ease and efficiency and much quicker than you ever could. It takes them two hours compared to your ten hours for the same activity.

***Your HouseCleaner***

It is very common for people to say 'I will get a housecleaner as soon as I can afford it'. The issue with that is that instead of spending time on revenue generating activities, they will spend hours and hours every week cleaning their house. To make matters worse, this is a total hamster wheel. Cleaning is never ending and is never complete. I am sometimes criticized for the lack of time I spend on cleaning. My motto is 'Why spend major time on minor things?' If a task is not generating revenue, delegate the activity. I suggest finding a housecleaner who is able to work with your budget. Often the two of you can come up with a compromise. If you have little money each week to spend on cleaning, just hire someone for an hour to tidy up and throw in a load of laundry.

Make a list of the cleaning activities that are most important to you. I suggest the ones that are regular activities, such as:

- Folding laundry.
- Changing bed sheets.
- Vacuuming and washing floors.
- Washing and drying dishes.
- Bathrooms/kitchen cleaning.

Next, you can interview some housecleaners in your area. Have your list ready for them and see if the two of you can come up with a price per hour to take care of these activities on a weekly basis. Even if they do not clean your entire house, you can delegate some of the 'time-stealers' that have to be done regularly.

### ***Your Virtual Assistant***

No, you are not dreaming! You can afford a virtual assistant. There is a booming business in the area of personal assistants that can work from their home. What is even more appealing is that you can search online for an assistant by location, skill set, and price.

### ***Hiring a Million Dollar Financial Advisor***

This step is very important. Most people will hire someone to take care of their money that is in the same financial situation that they are (or worse). First and foremost, it is important to be an excellent money manager yourself. If you are struggling with deciding where your money goes, or you just spend money until the cash runs out, even the best financial advisor cannot help you with your daily money ins and money outs. You must become an excellent money manager if you are not already. This means tracking where every dollar goes, and tracking what transactions take place each day for personal and business reasons.

When it comes to your finances, you should have your very own 'wealth' team. This includes your bookkeeper, you wealth coach and your financial advisor. When it comes to a financial advisor, I would recommend someone who is already a millionaire. It is also important to hire an advisor who is educated and familiar with creating multiple streams of income (not just investing in mutual funds and creating RRSP accounts). You want to hire an expert, and that means hiring someone who can help you invest in different ways. Interview your financial advisor! Do they have experience with real estate, business start-ups, and passive income streams? Do they have multiple streams of income themselves? What products do they represent? Do they only promote mutual funds? What types of returns can you expect from the different products they work with?

Where do you find these advisors? Ask around. Ask wealthy people for referrals! Email someone in business you admire and ask them who they use as an advisor. Ask around and you will stumble upon a handful of names. Many of these experts have financial credibility, and they would certainly, at the very least, be open to meeting with you. They may even offer you a great referral!

Actions Of The Day

1. Ask around for a highly recommended bookkeeper.

2. Ask around for a highly recommended house cleaner.

3. Ask around for a highly recommended virtual assistant or website where you can find a virtual assistant.

4. Read your 30-day goal.

## Day 29 - Health Is Your Money Magnet - Become a Well Preneur

Create a **wellpreneur revolution**! As a business owner, you are a walking, talking business card for your personal brand or business. It is critical that you recognize that your state of health will eventually either accelerate or hinder your business results. Too often, we get caught up in the momentum of our busy businesses and we put our personal health on the backburner. Over time, we end up doing the best we can to stay on top of things, but at the expense of our personal magnetism and energy. Not only will you be drained, but your business profits will eventually drain as well. Your health is your best and most valuable asset. You should be spending your most precious time and money taking care of yourself. Surround yourself with an expert team that you can rely on for personal care - your coaches, your mentors, your health practitioners. Build your very own 'power team' to help keep you accountable and help keep you at your very best.

**Your Personal Power Team Checklist:**

- Business Coach(es) / Mentor(s)
- Massage Therapist
- Health Practitioner(s)
- Nutritional Coach
- Great listeners/cheerleaders
- Beauty Experts (to help you look and feel your best)
- Personal Trainer / Yoga Instructor / Pilates Instructor
- Healer(s) / Therapist(s)
- Sport Coach (if you are an athlete)

It is a big team, but you have big ambitions and as an entrepreneur, you are exerting more personal energy, mental power and hours than most people. Remember, you are a walking, talking business card. If you do not feel your best, you will not reach your true potential.

Low-glycemic eating, taking supplements and exercising regularly is the optimal health triad I promote. Email us at info@healthygirl.net to receive your free HealthyGirl Grocery List. We are also happy to offer you a 15 minute free consultation should you require some support for nutrition and/or supplement suggestions.

Register for **HealthyGirl's Monthly Newsletter**, which focuses on entrepreneurship, optimal health and wealth building for women.

Actions Of The Day

1. Identify the members of your personal power team. Are there any gaps? Can you ask for a referral for an area that you may need some extra support?

2. Get in the habit of booking your fitness time in your dayplanner eight weeks in advance. Book it as a meeting, which cannot be cancelled.

3. Set a fitness goal for yourself for 2010 (run a 5K, do a triathlon, start yoga, walk outside daily...).

4. Make a morning ritual checklist (i.e. drink water, take vitamins, eat a low-glycemic breakfast). Create a new habit of following this checklist in the morning.

5. Book regular dates with yourself. This means scheduling time each week to do things just for you, such as goal setting, journaling, and reading. Sundays are a great time for this!

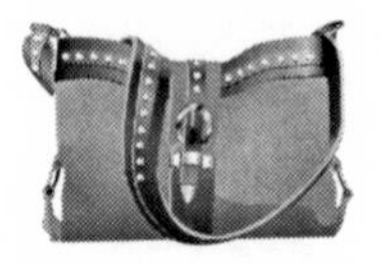

# Day 30- Million Dollar Summary Tips

Congrats on making it to Day 30! My intention when creating this program was to share some of the resources, trainings and tips that have helped accelerate my business and improve my health. I am truly grateful that you embarked on this program with me and I hope you can take away some key insights. Although this is our final day together, I truly hope you stay in touch. Please stay connected by joining our **HealthyGirl Facebook Group** and our **HealthyGirl Newsletter**.

To complete your 30-day program, here are a few tips that will be helpful for you to maintain your fabulous momentum, and to keep your business and your health moving forward in a positive direction. Granted, you will surely hit some rough patches and some tough days, but know that we all do. Leaders learn to discipline their disappointments and pick themselves up a little faster each time. Practice this! I promise you, within a year, you will really notice that you recover quickly and that your personal and business life will flourish.

1. Surround yourself with an incredible team, for business and for health.
2. Find a mentor (or a few mentors). I suggest 'Millionaire Mentors'!
3. As of today, jump out of your comfort zone and quit living comfortably.
4. Be clear about the vision you are creating for yourself, and look at your vision board daily.
5. Become an excellent goal-setter. Set 30-day goals often, and make a goal book each year. Be careful not to set too many

goals in one period.

6. Read your "Financial Freedom Date" often and keep up with those post-it notes!
7. Put pictures of what you want on the ceiling of your bedroom. You will be amazed at what happens.
8. Read 'Think & Grow Rich' and 'The Power of the Subconscious Mind' often; they are reference books and should be read over and over again.
9. Take personal days for yourself. Book a one day retreat when you need to refuel!
10. Read every day.
11. Unleash your ability to lead. Stop living small. You live only once.
12. Build a Brand. Create a Tribe. Be Bold. Give Value. Just Do It!
13. Leverage social media or leverage experts. Create a great presence online. Blog. Post comments on other blogs or community sites.
14. Attend events. Become a student. Make your car your university.
15. Learn to discipline your disappointments.
16. Think and Act like a Millionaire before the money comes.
17. Remember - Profits Are Better Than Wages!
18. Create multiple streams of income.
19. Educate yourself on the power of passive income. Get on the passive income train.
20. Interview and have coffee with successful people. Learn from them.
21. Start to create Leverage for yourself with time and money. Stop doing everything yourself. Stop overworking and over exerting.
22. Stop working for less than you are worth. Be confident and communicate to others what you are worth.
23. Become an excellent money manager (i.e. manage your cash flow, net worth statements).
24. Hire a bookkeeper, virtual assistant and a housecleaner.
25. Stop taking your health for granted. Take care of yourself. What good is the money you make if you are an unhealthy,

sick and burned out entrepreneur.

26. Stop wasting so much time on the email (This is a tough one!).
27. Check in with yourself a few times a day. Are you running on empty? Are you out of fuel? Take some time out to refuel and take care of yourself.
28. Stop wasting your time on activities that do not generate money. Remember, what is the ROI (return on investment) for all the daily activities you do?
29. Inspire and mentor others. Share your key learning's with others. Be generous with sharing your knowledge and experience. Pay it forward.
30. Give back. Use the wealth you are generating for yourself to create opportunities for others and to keep the money circulating! Be generous with your wonderful wealth.

# Join the HealthyGirl Community!

## HealthyGirl's 30 Days to Wealth Seminar Series

In 2010, **HealthyGirl's 30 Days to Wealth Seminar** is coming to a city near you. Be sure to check our events page on our website and to register for our newsletter, so that you can be one of the first to be informed. These events will be exclusive VIP events, and will have limited seating. The "Kick-Off Seminar" was held in Toronto, Canada on Feb 27, 2009. New dates are being added throughout 2010 and 2011.

## HealthyGirl's Monthly Newsletter

Join our **monthly newsletter** and keep in touch! Be among the first to be informed of great products, events and information that will support your journey as a wellpreneur!

## HealthyGirl's Facebook Group

Join our growing **HealthyGirl facebook** group to keep in touch and network with other members of the HealthyGirl Community.

**www.healthygirl.ca**

**Suggested Books and References List:**

The Top 10 Distinctions Between Millionaires and the Middle Class - Keith Cameron Smith

Think and Grow Rich - Napoleon Hill

The Science of Getting Rich - Wallace D Wattles

Money For Life Presentation - Richard Brooks (www.richardbrooks.com)

The 4-Hour Workweek - Timothy Ferriss

The Millionaire Maker's Guide to Wealth Cycle Investing - Loral Langemeier

The Millionaire Maker - Loral Langemeier

Cash Machine - Loral Langemeier

Guide to Becoming Rich - Robert Kiyosaki

Rich Dad, Poor Dad - Robert Kiyosaki

Secrets of the Millionaire Mind - T Harv Eker

Multiple Streams of Income - Robert Allen

The Power of the Subconscious Mind - Dr Joseph Murphy

You Were Born Rich - Bob Proctor

The Magic of Believing - Clive Bristol

The E-Myth Revisited: Why Most Small Businesses Don't Work and What To Do About It - Michael E Gerber

Success Magazine (www.success.com)

Multiple Streams of Income - Robert Allen

The Success Principles - Jack Canfield

Why We Want You To Be Rich - Donald Trump and Robert Kiyosaki

Speed Wealth - T Harv Eker

Tribes - Seth Godin

The Next Millionaires - Paul Zane Pilzer

The New Glucose Revolution - Dr Jennie Brand-Miller

Ask and It Is Given - Esther Hicks

# COACHING PROGRAM

Based on the strategies and principles in '30 Days to Wealth', Leanne has put together a mentoring program to support your journey to reducing debt, creating more cash flow and creating your wealthy mindset. This mentoring program has been created to be intimate in size and to kick-start your wealth journey with the support and mentorship required to make positive financial changes in your life.

**Is the Coaching Program Right for you?**

Are you seeking support with reducing debt?
Are you seeking a success mentor?
Do you want to change your financial patterns?
Do you want to be on an accelerated wealth plan?
Are you an entrepreneur looking to accelerate profits?
Do you spend more than you make?
Are you living paycheck to paycheck?
Are you seeking to double or triple your cash flow?
Do you want to create financial independence?

**What's included in the Program?**

2 Intimate Group Sessions (60 minutes each).
Personal Coaching Session
Net Worth Accelerator
Personalized Wealth Accelerator Tracker

(Spaces are limited for each Session)
**Visit healthygirl.net**

Coaching Notes

LaVergne, TN USA
04 March 2011
218809LV00001B/124/P